D0887554

From Breakdown to Breakthrough

How the Devil Lost Again

From Breakdown to Breakthrough

John Jackson

From Breakdown to Breakthrough

How the Devil Lost Again

John Jackson

From Breakdown to Breakthrough

John Jackson

Library of Congress Cataloging–In–Publication Data

Name: Jackson, John, author.
Title: From Breakdown to Breakthrough/ John Jackson

Identifiers:
LCCN 2021913071

ISBN: 978-1-63960-003-8 Paperback
        978-1-63960-016-8 Hardcover
        978-1-63960-002-1 eBook

Published in the United States by Pen2Pad Ink Publishing.

Requests to publish work from this book or to contact the author should be sent to: jjloves2sing@yahoo.com

John Jackson retains the rights to all images.

From Breakdown to Breakthrough

Acknowledgements

First, I would like to dedicate this book to my Lord and Savior, Jesus Christ. You saw me fall time and time again, and You allowed me to triumph through it all.

A special thanks to my children, Jonicia Sharda' (deceased), Elijah De'Shod, Ja'Kyla Myrtise, and Carribean Lanai Jackson, who love me unconditionally.

To my parents, Elroy and Jo Ann Davis: Thanks for everything! You two are the BEST!

To my dad, John Fields: I love you so much.

To my sister, Kamisha Jackson, who has ALWAYS stood by her big brother's side: Thanks, Lil' Sis, and YES! We made it!

To the former Disciples of New Harvest Kingdom Church International (Dallas and

El Dorado) and the Destiny Empowerment Worship Center (DEW Center): Thanks for praying me through some of the roughest and toughest times of my life. Whew!

To my leaders, Apostle Sherman Cee Gee Allen and Co-Pastor Otonya Allen: Thanks for your unwavering love and support. It really means a lot to me.

To Apostle Shawn and Prophetess Yolanda Stephens: Thank you all so much for coming into my life and teaching me so much. The both of you are truly God sent, and I will never forget all that you've taught me and imparted into me! I love you guys dearly.

To my REAL friends who stayed by my side when the FAKES walked away: Thanks for being dependable and allowing me to be myself!

To my ministry supporters: Thank you for believing in me even when I sometimes didn't believe in myself. It is because of you that this book has come into fruition. Thanks for pushing me and letting me know that my very words, messages, songs, and existence means so much to you and blesses your life. I'm just glad to be a vessel for God.

Last, but certainly not least, I dare not forget my haters: THANKS FOR BEING MY GREATEST SUPPORTERS!

From Breakdown to Breakthrough

John Jackson

Introduction

On October 27, 2007, I was speaking with a friend about the things God was dealing with me about as it relates to a song and a message series entitled "Lord, Work On Me." It was through the mouth of that Prophet that the Lord spoke to me and said, "THAT'S A BOOK!" I realized and confirmed then that I was pregnant with triplets: a message series, a song, and now a book.

God is not pleased with those of us who have helped others in the delivery room to "push" and give birth to their destiny and dreams while the very baby that we've carried to full term lies dormant and/or dead in our bellies. Miscarriage, in every essence of the word, is not a good feeling. Something on the inside dies prematurely because of either natural cause, self-inflicted reasons, or many other exterior circumstances. However, the end of the process is "death." Another form of premature death is "abortion." It is to end life intentionally to a fetus that has been living due to the conception of a child. We

11

do the same when we inhibit God from using us to do His work and will.

I have had a few spiritual miscarriages as well as a few spiritual abortions. However, I am thankful to my Lord and Savior, Jesus Christ, that He did not shut up my womb and make me barren because of my disobedience. Instead, He gave me another chance to experience pregnancy and thereby give birth to my destiny.

This book is just one of many that God will allow me to give birth to. I pray this book takes root in your spirit and causes you to ultimately be blessed in the end.

Who Am I?

My name is Apostle John "JJ" Jackson, and I am so blessed to share my very first book with you. I look forward to what God is going to do through me. As I share my spiritual insight and real-life experiences, I hope to inspire you. It is my prayer that you are blessed, encouraged, and inspired.

I was born in Monroe, Louisiana to Jo Ann Jackson and John Willie Fields, Jr., but I grew up between Louisiana and Arkansas. How is that possible? Well, I lived in El Dorado, Arkansas, but most of my family lived in Spearsville, Lillie, and Bernice, Louisiana. These are small towns that are all approximately 30-35 miles from El Dorado. Don't get it twisted: These small towns produce some very brilliant and strong individuals. As a grown man, I can proudly admit that the travels back and forth across the Louisiana-Arkansas state line were some of the best days of my life. I grew up with elders who taught me respect for myself and others. Oh, how I miss the good old days with my wonderful family and friends.

I grew up in a very close-knit family. We saw everyone on a weekly basis. We loved to go to Grandma's house so that we could eat, play softball, and go to church. We were taught to never disrespect or talk back to our elders. LIE, DARN, and FOOL were three of many words that, if spoken aloud, could get you a good lashing from Grandma or one of my aunts. As a matter of fact, those three words are still outlawed in my family today. My mom will still pop me upside my head if she hears me say any of those words (I'm for real).

I grew up in Beech Grove Baptist Church in Spearsville, LA. Every member of the church was also a family member. My cousins and I loved to sing in the choir. We really thought we had made it when we started wearing our black bottom and white top uniforms.

I started singing around five years old, and I have loved music ever since. Eventually, I became the musician for the church. I would beat on that old piano all day and night, and I loved every minute of it. Sometimes, I would practice while my grandmother, aunts, and other family members would be there cleaning up the church. I would make up songs and experiment with the choir. Fortunately, they did not mind at all.

People started recognizing my gift of music, so they started to put me on the program at all the local musicals and concerts. I probably sang at almost every black church around Spearsville and El Dorado. All I wanted to do was sing, sing, sing. I would sing until the tears would roll down my face. I could feel the presence of God flowing through me as I ministered in song even as a child. I didn't know it then but singing at Beech Grove Baptist Church was the start of something that would one day allow me to sing all over the world.

My humble beginnings led me to singing in big concerts and stages in front of gospel celebrities. I have appeared on shows such as *BET's Sunday Best*, *Bobby Jones Gospel* and *Amateur Night* at the Apollo in Harlem, NY. God has favored me. I'm amazed, grateful, and humbled. I'm even more thankful for my family that pushed me to keep singing and seeking a closer walk with God even when I didn't want to.

My childhood was great. My mom and other relatives did all they could to take care of me and protect me. However, there is only so much that a parent can do. After that, the enemy goes on the prowl.

I knew something was special and different about me. I never felt comfortable around a lot of people. I never fit in with the "good ol' boys." No matter what I did or how hard I tried, it just never worked for me. Now, I realize that God had His hand on me. There was an anointing on my life even as a child. It would not let me mingle with any and everybody (I will admit that I did try).

God has been good to me. He has allowed me to experience much of what others only dreamed about. That's the good part. As you read in this book, however, you will find I have faced many "valley" experiences. Contrary to popular belief, my life is nowhere near perfect. I have, however, managed to overcome and keep moving forward just like you. Some of it has been very bad and embarrassing. Still, I wouldn't change it for anything because my maturity has improved in Christ. I understand that even the chaos and craziness was for my good. Romans 8:28 (KJV) states, *And we know that ALL things work together for good to them that love God, to them who are called according to his purpose.*

I have traveled across the United States and abroad singing and preaching to all who will listen. I've always been a person who never gave up on what I wanted in life. I am a firm believer that, if you want something out of life, then you've got to go after it. Never accept NO for an answer even if you fail the first time or the second time. Never give up and keep pursuing until you reach your manifested dreams and goals. I am a stubborn person, and I do not consider that to be a bad thing. I can have the whole world against me. That's fine. The world better be prepared for a fight with my determination.

All I've gone through in my life has been in alignment with the will of God. Although we don't always understand, we must accept what God allows and keep moving forward toward the destiny God has for us: THE GREATER THE MESS, THE GREATER THE MESSAGE. And oh, have I gone through some mess! This book is an excerpt of my life along with spiritual revelations that the Father gave me to share with all who will read. I pray that as you read this book you will allow the words of the Holy Spirit, as well as my life experiences, to unlock the potential in you. Doing so will help you to overcome and move forward in your life no matter what your obstacles may be. The Bible declares in Psalms 34:19 (KJV) that *Many are the afflictions of the righteous, but the Lord delivereth them out of them ALL.* I am a living witness that He will not just do it one time, but He will continually do it over and over again.

The struggle in the church is phenomenal. There are so many self-righteous Saints, 'aints', and pranks who act as if some issues discussed in this book are "non-existent." That devil is a liar! The struggle is ALIVE AND THRIVING. It will continue to be until we expose the truth about REAL LIFE ISSUES! I'm not acting as if I've arrived, but I am one with a daily prayer to God saying, "LORD, WORK ON ME."

Chapter 1

Lord, Work on Me

(THE ACKNOWLEDGEMENT OF SIN)

For all have sinned and come short of the glory of God.

~Romans 3:23 (KJV)

One of the greatest weapons the enemy uses on the saved as well as the unsaved is the weapon of "blinded eyes." For the unsaved, "blinded eyes" is the fact of being lost in sin and not even realizing that deliverance and salvation is needed in their life. For the saved, "blinded eyes" is the fact of pointing out other people's problems and flaws and not seeing or acknowledging their own sins, struggles, and/or shortcomings. Regardless if you are saved or unsaved, whenever there is a need for deliverance in any area of our lives, we must be able to free ourselves from what others may think of us. We must learn to just stop and say, "Lord, work on me."

Anytime I make the statement that my car needs to be worked on, I am implying that something in my car is malfunctioning and needs to be fixed. Something is causing the dysfunction. Likewise, when you say, "Lord, work on me," you are acknowledging that there is something in your life that is out of alignment, broken, and/or needs fixing.

As Saints of God, we need to be real with ourselves. All of us have some things that need to be worked on. Even on our best day, we are still as dirty rags (Isaiah 64:6). Even as you read this book now, ask yourself: *What is it that I need to work on in my life?* I believe that we must constantly evaluate ourselves and our spiritual state to see what has become weak and worn. As the writer Paul said, *Brethren, I count not myself to have apprehended; but this one thing I do, forgetting those things which are behind, and reaching forth unto those things which are before, I press toward the mark for the prize of the high calling of God in Christ Jesus.* Philippians 3:13-14 (KJV)

There must be a constant pressing in our spirit to be all that God has called us to be in these last and evil days. Many people die and leave earth with unfulfilled callings, anointings, assignments, duties, etc. I constantly ask God to work on me so that I may become all that He wants me to be. My prayer is always that God would keep me humble so that I may never get to the point of thinking that 'I have arrived'. I am amazed and sometimes shocked at the many self-righteous and stuck-up saints I meet who are always quick to look down on others but overlook their own weaknesses and flaws.

God,

Work on me so that I may not EVER become one of them. I don't want to spend the rest of my life always looking for the beam in other people's eyes and miss the opportunity for God to show me the beam in mine.

We must be very careful when constantly gossiping and murmuring about the struggles, failures, shortcomings, and downfall of others. That is how the enemy gets us caught up. We lose focus on *us* and start focusing on *them*! All of us are one step from a scandal, divorce, bankruptcy, an unwanted pregnancy, a sexually transmitted disease (STD), and/or the loss of everything. It is the grace and mercy of God and the blood of Jesus that covers us in the midst of whatever our weaknesses are. Many are guilty of the same thing that others have been exposed for, but the only reason you are still in it is because you didn't get caught! (Now let the church say A-M-E-N!)

My recent transitions revealed that many people are so judgmental and forget that they have gone through some transitions publicly and/or privately. I am so thankful that God has seen fit to choose me to be an example to the saved as well as the unsaved. Whether it be through my failures or my successes, I believe that the Father is using me to be an example to all. I don't profess to be without error, struggle, or mistakes. I do love the Lord with all my heart and soul. I constantly have to stay in His presence, so He can do the work that needs to be done *in* me, *on* me, and *through* me. The time is done for Men and Women of God to appear *perfect* before people but *pitiful* in private. Let me be the first to say that without me staying in the presence of God: I AM A MESS! *God, continue to work on me because I truly desire to be a vessel sanctified for Your use.*

Why am I speaking like this? I believe that God assigned me to be a voice to the nations and to expose the devil. If we, as men and women of God, are going to draw the world to Christ, we must first let them know major constructions and cleanups have taken place in our own personal lives. We need to be transparent about our lives and some of the things that God has brought us through and delivered us from. I also believe that many others would come to Christ when we start telling them the truth about where God really brought us from. You may see me dancing and shouting now, lifting Holy hands, living the blessed life, and hear me singing Zion songs now, but do you *really* know where I came from?

Many people are not saved and not in church because of what they've seen in previous leaders: fake and phony people that model Christianity as if it is a life of no problems, stresses, or struggles. I've seen those phony people cast down and cast out others for things that were done openly, but they commit those same sins and/or acts privately! I have a problem with those phony people who down others for whatever it is that they are doing wrong, but in private they try to do those acts with them (Some of you will catch that tomorrow… humph!). Don't get me wrong, I'm not by any means condoning sin, but I believe that the Word of God is for all and will stand through all. The Word of God is a guide for God's vessels and God's followers equally. At the end of the day, it's still *holiness* or *hell*!

When was the last time you asked God for a spiritual makeover? When you look in your spiritual mirror, what do you see? Is it pretty? Is it ugly? Could you use some changes for the better? B. Slade, formerly known as Tonex, sang a song on one of his projects that said, "Make me over, again." My version of his powerful words is "God, do a complete makeover in me." For so long, I've heard folk be "churchy" and say, "If you find anything that shouldn't be, take it out and strengthen me." I'm going to say, "When you find it, take it out and strengthen me. I am not all that God would have me to be, but I am a yielded vessel that is willing to allow You to do a makeover in me."

Regardless of your title, denomination, religious affiliation, or even your tenure of salvation, YOU still need to ask God to CONTINUALLY work on those things in your life that are not in perfect alignment with His will. I'm always amazed at these super religious and overly emotional people. It's sad, but many people will never be healed, delivered, and set free from the issues that plague them because they will always assume that they have to "act" a certain way before others so no one will think negatively about them and/or their walk with God.

Love not the world, neither the things that are in the world. If any man loves the world, the love of the Father is not in him. For all that is in the world, the lust of the flesh, and the lust of the eyes, and the pride of life, is not of the Father, but is of the world

~I John 2:15-16

The five senses (taste, touch, smell, hearing, and seeing) all report to the carnal mind which is the enemy of God. Satan uses these senses to tempt us! The lust of the flesh includes tasting, touching, smelling, and hearing. The lust of the eyes is seeing. The pride of life is thinking you are special because of who you are, what you have, what you know, or what you look like. The enemy uses these three things, the lust of the flesh, the lust of the eyes and the pride of life, to entice us to sin. Scripture shows this process at work in both the Garden of Eden and on the Mount of Temptation with Jesus in the fourth chapter of Matthew.

You may be reading this book and feel as if you are so flawed that you can never be forgiven, and God can never use you. Let me be the first to tell you that is so far from the truth. In fact, when you research the 12 disciples of Jesus Christ, many of them had a past and/or an issue.

The 12 apostles were disciples of Jesus Christ during his earthly ministry almost 2,000 years ago. Jesus picked each of the apostles. None of them chose Jesus until He first chose them. Jesus didn't choose them based on social status, intelligence, spiritual maturity, or personalities. He chose them for his own reasons and purpose. Even though Jesus chose the 12 disciples, they still had flaws and failures just like everybody else. They weren't holier than anybody else was then or today. Judas Iscariot betrayed Jesus for 30 pieces of silver. Peter denied Jesus. Thomas was a doubter. God still chose them for His purpose.

Some may argue with me to say that I am promoting failures among God's people, but I am not. My purpose is to simply inspire and encourage you, the reader, who may feel as if you can't be used by God because of past failures, present struggles, and future fears. If God can use a curser and a fighter like Peter, He can use you and me! I am thankful for how God has been transforming my life and allowing me to see things through His eyes and not just mine. I believe that God will conduct spiritual surgeries for all who will acknowledge that there is a spiritual infection internally that will eventually poison the spirit if not removed. We need to stop focusing solely on what is right in our lives and start looking for the things that we are keeping under the rug! (Somebody will get that tomorrow.)

What are you holding on to that God is not pleased with? What is it that you keep thinking will just go away one day, but you find yourself struggling and fighting alone? What is it or who is it that God has been trying to deliver you from, but you keep saying, "Not now Lord, but later"? Acknowledge the struggles and weaknesses.

That is the first step in moving toward freedom from bondage of whatever it is. Many times, the enemy wants us to overlook the fact that we are really jacked up. He wants us to hide the very thing that can and will destroy us. In the words of Apostle Shawn Stephens, "When you expose yourself, then you take the authority from the devil to do so." Since no one knows the day or hour when the son of man shall appear, now is the time to lift your hands and say, "LORD WORK ON ME!"

Chapter 2

Lord, Work on My Mind

And be not conformed to this world: but be ye transformed by the renewing of your mind...

~Romans 12:2 (KJV)

I've often heard people say that "The mind is a terrible thing to waste." Now that I have grown in Christ, I understand that statement and why people say it. The mind is a battleground. The enemy will usually attack the minds of people. The enemy recognizes that if he has our minds then we are too weak to fight. He has the upper hand. I must admit that the devil once had full control of my mind. Thanks be to God who gives me the victory. I am free in my mind right now!

There were times when I battled in my

mind with thoughts of committing suicide. One night when I was in college, I became so frustrated, mad, and overwhelmed with life's circumstances that I planned to end my life. I decided that I was going to overdose on multiple medications. The enemy had my mind. His plan was to use me to take myself out. *But God! Hallelujah! I feel a shout in my spirit even as I write this.* God came down and gave me peace of mind.

With the pills in my hands, God sent a sense of relief into my spirit. I dropped the pills on the floor and started sobbing. I felt like I let God down. I was ministering God's word and singing His praises, but I was about to end my life. I was selfish to try to make a permanent decision based upon temporary circumstances. The bible says, *Thou wilt keep him in perfect peace, whose mind is stayed upon thee.* (Isaiah 26:3 (KJV)). I had no peace because my mind did not stay on Jesus.

With all the gifts that God gave me, somewhere along the road I didn't guard the gates of my mind. So, the enemy got in. All the devil was looking for was an entry way into my spirit. What better way to get in than through the mind? After all, the mind is the central system to all our innermost thoughts. Why would he attack my mind? It is because everything we see before us in the natural world starts from a thought. How many of your dreams died because the enemy interrupted your thought process with negativity? Maybe you were thinking about starting your own business, but the devil made you think that it would not be successful. He's a LIAR! Maybe you thought about going back to school and completing your diploma or degree, but the enemy made you think that you were too old or too dumb. The devil is still a LIAR! Maybe you were going to focus on your Kingdom Assignment, but the enemy made you think that it could NEVER happen or come to pass for you. Again, the devil is a LIAR! Maybe you were thinking of writing a book, but the enemy caused you to second guess yourself. The devil is LIAR!

The mind is a battleground. It's the place where, if allowed, the enemy will kill your destiny, your assignments, and your dreams. The enemy will pollute our mind with negativity and carnal thoughts. Romans 8: 6-7 (KJV) explains the benefits of a spirit filled mind:

For to be carnally minded is death, but to be spiritually minded is life and peace. Because the carnal mind is enmity against God: for it is not subject to the law of God, neither indeed can be.

What better place is there for the devil to try to destroy us than on the battleground of our mind? How many times did the enemy get you into a carnal mindset and the result was destruction, pain, and/or hurt? How many times have you failed a course of life because your body was in classroom training, but your mind was playing hooky and having fun on the other side of town?

Many today are suffering physically and spiritually from carnal decisions that were made years ago. The end result of a carnal mind is death. This is the reason the devil keeps haunting and battling with you in your mind. I declare and decree now that you will have total victory!

God is now raising a generation of believers that is going to walk in total victory over their mind. We must be wise enough to cast down every thought that is not like God. I am now comfortable with saying that I really have lost my mind. I had to lose my mind in order that I may gain the mind of Christ.

Let this mind be in you, which was also in Christ Jesus
                    ~Philippians 2:5

Now that I have a new mind, my thoughts have changed. I think of the greater things in God. So, for all those people who said that I had lost my mind: Thank you! You finally told the truth.

As a born-again believer, you must lose your carnal (fleshly or worldly) mind in order to obtain the mind of Christ. The carnal mind cannot comprehend the things of God. If we are going to be truly in tune with God and his assignments for our lives, there must be a total mind change.

In July 2004, the Lord told me to move from the bustling city of Little Rock back to my hometown of El Dorado to start my ministry. If I was not listening to God's will for me, I would have stayed in Little Rock. My carnal mind was telling me that I was only 3 weeks away from starting law school in Little Rock. On the other hand, my spiritual mind had taken total control. I knew if God was calling me to move back to El Dorado, then He already had things worked out on my behalf.

My family and I moved back to El Dorado and began the ministry. Because of our obedience to the will of God, we experienced blessings like never before. Those blessings only came because of our willingness to submit our mind into the total control and the will of God for our lives. You may be reading this book and wrestling with your mind as to what you're going to do next! Well, it's simple: Do what God is telling you to do. Stop trying to figure out the outcome. Remember that *...my thoughts are not your thoughts, neither are your ways my ways, saith the Lord. For as the heavens are higher than the earth, so are my ways higher than your ways and my thoughts than your thoughts. ~ Isaiah 55: 8-9 (KJV)*

If we're not careful, then our minds will play tricks on us. Open your mouth and say the following with me regardless of where you are: "I've been tricked in my mind for the last time!"

"Out with the Old and In with the New"

If you are going to fully embrace what God has for you, you've got to learn how to get the victory *in* and *over* your mind. Many will never come to receive intended blessings because they try to obtain the things of God with "old" mindsets. There must be a cleansing of the mind that washes out any negative thoughts that fight against your purpose and destiny. Old thoughts cannot go where God is taking you right now. Old thoughts are the thoughts that make you feel inadequate, unworthy, and even at times unashamed. These negative and dirty thoughts made us feel like our sin was alright. These old mindsets fed negativity and doubt. These old mindsets did not challenge us to strive for perfection and excellence. These old mindsets allowed us to sin without feeling any sense of conviction. This is the very reason why I say, "Out with the old and in with the new."

God wants to give every person that yields themselves to Him a brand-new heart and mind. Your new mindset will think on things that are holy and pure:

Finally, brethren, whatsoever things are true, whatsoever things are honest, whatsoever things are just, whatsoever things are pure, whatsoever things are lovely, whatsoever things are of good report; if there be any virtue, and if there be any praise, think on these things.

~Philippians 4:8 (KJV).

Many people are seeking and asking God for new things and places, but they still possess the same old mindset! What difference would it make to be in a new place and/or have new things and still have the same old mindset? You take that same old mentality to that new place and get the same results as you had before you received your new thing or place. It's like the children of Israel taking their slavery mentality into the land God promised them. How do you want the blessings of the promised land, but you also want to hold on to the mindset of Egypt? It does not line up.

My idea of having a new house is also to have new furniture to go into my new house. One day, when my house is built from the ground up (I'm certain it is on the way.), I don't want to take the old furniture that I have now into my new place. Why? It will be misplaced and will not match up to the new place. I must upgrade. Elevation must take place.

We are quick to ask God for elevation, but we do not really realize that it's going to require more from us on our end. We rush to the stores to get the latest gadgets being put on the market, but we forget that it will probably cost more or require more of our time to operate I remember looking at a segment on one of the local news stations where people waited in line for hours and days to get the updated iPhone, shoes, televisions, etc. How is it that we want everything upgraded in the natural, but we don't want to upgrade our mentality? Some of you right now have a floor model mentality, but you want an HD flat screen manifestation. You must upgrade in this season and this hour. You can no longer possess the same old mindset. God seeks to do more in your life. There is absolutely nothing wrong with wanting more in your life, but please understand that *To whom much is given much is required.* (Luke 12:48 (KJV))

You will not be able to operate as you

once did with your old mindset. Everything that God is preparing for us is going to be so BIG and great in Him that our natural minds will not even be able to believe it! I know you have wrestled back and forth in the storms of life. You've struggled back and forth in your mind on what you should do and where you should go. You are wondering how you're going to do it.

God is saying that He's going to elevate your blessings and allow manifestation to hit your life. Some of you reading this book have literally been called crazy by others who did not see what you saw or did not feel what you felt in the spirit. They even talked about you. That happened because they were blind to what God is getting ready to do in your life. I promise that you were not just seeing and hearing things. God was showing you a glimpse of your future and your destiny. It's going to be great for you! Keep thinking positive. Keep allowing God to show himself strong in your life. Don't you dare carry your old mentality into your new place! I decree and declare that you'll never ever go back to your old mindset and your old ways of thinking. Your old mentality fed you with doubt and fear. You have now tapped into a whole new dimension, and you will see just how great things are getting ready to happen in your life.

"Guard Your Mind"

It is vitally important that you GUARD YOUR MIND! The enemy is sneaky. Sometimes he uses a disguise as he creeps his way into your mind. It's very important to sensor everything that enters your thought process. He finds the place in your mind that is unguarded or unprotected. Then, he enters and takes full control.

You must guard your mind by censoring what you see (VISION), say (VOICE) and what you sanction (VALIDATE).

I believe that it is also vitally important that we CENSOR WHAT WE SEE! Many people are battling and struggling now in their minds because they did not censor what they beheld with their eyes!

Genesis 3:6 (KJV) explains how Eve's eyes caused her AND us pain we did not deserve:

And when the woman saw that the tree was good for food, and that it was pleasant to the eyes, and a tree to be desired to make one wise, she took off the fruit thereof, and did eat, and gave also unto her husband with her; and he did eat.

It's important to note that Eve's experience of what she *saw* stimulated her and caused her to desire something that she was NOT supposed to have. From that point, it influenced her behavior to operate in disobedience.

What did you *see* or *view* with your eyes that opened up the window and gave power to the battles and struggles that you now have in your mind? Was it something in person? On the internet? On television? In a book? Only YOU know the real answer to this question! Whatever it was, go back to the root and deal with it so that you can walk in total victory and receive the manifested blessings of the promises that God has for you! You are a champion! Always remember that!

Many adults today are struggling in their mind because of negative seeds that were planted as a child. Maybe you watched your father beat your mother, and now you struggle with that today. Maybe you were introduced to video pornography or magazine pornography as a child, and now the spirit of lust is manifesting in your life today.

Whatever you have seen in your past that has negatively impacted and affected your life, it must be released today. My experiences taught me that we cannot change the past or even the things that we viewed in our past. However, we can allow God to give us a new perspective in place of the old negative perspective that the enemy has left imprinted in our spirits.

I saw things as a child that I should have never seen. I had to decide if I was going to keep repeating it or release it in order to get the victory for me! The choice was mine. Did I do everything right? NO! Did I miss the mark at times? Absolutely! Thanks be to God! He continually gives all of us the victory through it all. We must censor what we see. When we do this, we'll see greater results and manifestations in our life, and we will also block off another entry way that the enemy uses to destroy us. Remember, you are a champion, and ALWAYS remember that!

"My Testimony of The Mind"

Wow! Where exactly do I begin? Many people may look at me and think that I've always been perfect. I've never experienced any mind battling circumstances! I wish that was all true. My life has been far from the "perfect life." I do not expect you to get on the phone or in a group to gossip and make me the center of your conversation. It is to inspire and encourage all. I want to let you know that no matter how bad things look and how you are battling in your mind, YOU CAN RECOVER!

If you want to see someone who knows what it feels like to actually lose their mind, I AM HE! In an attempt to end my problems and supposedly make things easier for myself and others, I suffered a nervous breakdown and attempted suicide. WHAT! This was not supposed to be something that would happen to JOHN JACKSON. Guess what? It did!

I was placed in the hospital for several days. They flushed out my system with some charcoal looking stuff that I NEVER and I repeat NEVER want to taste again. After being released from the hospital, I thought I was going home. Instead, I was transported by the police to a mental institution in order to be evaluated and treated. The doctors and nurses felt that I would harm myself again.

I arrived at this mental health institution. An intake person greeted me. In my mind, I kept saying, *Now I feel like I'm in prison. I can't believe it. Me. John Jackson. Singer. Preacher. God's faithful servant. In "the crazy house."* I never dreamed that I would have a nervous breakdown.

God was still dealing with me my first night there. I sat up on my bed all night writing a song. I didn't even understand why. I was mad at God, my family, and everyone. I didn't want to pray. I didn't want to read my bible or anything. I just wanted to DIE! Truly, my mind was gone!

Some patients rammed their heads into walls. Some ran down the hallway at full speed like someone was chasing them. They even had some that screamed and cried, "My insides are on fire!"

How in the world did I end up in this place?! I allowed the enemy to do destructive work on my mind. Even in all of this, God spoke to me: *Look around this room at these people. You still have it better.* I am in a mental institution, and God is telling me that I still have it better! I was in the place of chaos and crazy, but there was still someone else that was in a far worse situation and circumstance than me!

I was diagnosed with Major Depression. The doctors prescribed medications for my nerves, my anxiety, and my sleep. Trust me, I know what it's like to be on medications in order to function throughout the day and have a little peace of mind. Many of you are reading this now, and you feel like you are at your wits end! Let me be the first to tell you that as bad as it looks, you still have it better!

No matter how crazy I may get, music can find me anywhere. God made sure it could find me even when I was not in my right mind. The recreation room in the institution had a piano. I sat down and started playing. Eventually, I started singing. Before I knew it, every single patient was in the room listening. Some had silent tears rolling down their cheeks. Even the nurses and technicians joined in on the worship experience. I thought that these people needed their medication. In actuality, God used me to reach them in my moment of psychiatric displacement.

When I finished, people came up to me. They expressed their desire to rededicate their lives to Christ. One of those people, a young black girl named Virginia, told me something that completely surprised me: "You are not in here for yourself. God sent you here for all of us." Wow. I cried and thanked God for using me. No, I didn't understand His why, but I'm grateful for it. He took my bad and made it for His glory!

And we know that all things work together for good to them that love God, to them who are called according to his purpose.

~Romans 8:28 (KJV)

ALL of this took place after I got saved. I was still in ministry leading God's people. It's so easy for everyone to look at Pastors and leaders and assume that all is well in our lives. We need prayer just like everyone else.

I was released into the hands of my family who nurtured me, prayed for me, and continued to encourage me. I required monitoring after being released because at certain times I would feel myself about to wig out! I couldn't tolerate loud noises and couldn't really be around a lot of people. LOOK AT GOD NOW!!!

I'm a living testimony. When destiny is upon your life, the devil will try everything, but it just won't work. I'm a witness to all that may be going through the same situation. God can change your circumstances. If I had to preach a message on the attack of my mind, I would entitle it, "FROM BREAK DOWN TO BREAKTHROUGH: THE DEVIL LOST AGAIN!!!"

My prayer is that you understand that the enemy is out to destroy your mind just as he tried to destroy mine. Don't be so quick to judge people who have had nervous breakdowns and/or who have attempted to commit suicide. Remember that if your mind is unguarded, then you too are one circumstance away from a breakdown.

Chapter 3

Lord, Work on My Mouth

Death and life are in the power of the tongue: and they that love it shall eat the fruit thereof.

~*Proverbs 18:21 (KJV)*

Many people experience events in their life because of the words that they speak out of their mouths due to ignorance. Many are playing out roles they never intended to play, but it's an act of what you have spoken. In other words, it is vitally important that we monitor every word because those same words create and shape our world and lives. This is possible because of the authority and power given to us through our tongue.

In the past, I spoke things I really did not mean. As a result, many of those things have come to pass in my life. I have experienced the good, the bad, and the ugly based on those very words.

Do NOT *speak* what you do not want to manifest! Stop *speaking* that you are broke. Stop *speaking* that you are sick. Stop *speaking* that your marriage will never get better. Stop *speaking* that you won't get the job or the promotion. Stop *speaking* that you won't be approved for the house! All these words will eventually shape your future. Many people don't truly understand how much power has been given unto us from our Father (God).

Death and life are in the power of the tongue, and they that love it shall eat the fruit thereof.

~Proverbs 18:21 (KJV)

This scripture applies to all: saved and unsaved. Let's look at that scripture again. The first three words read, "Death and life..." In other words, NEGATIVE and POSITIVE are both created by what we speak. The scripture proceeds to say, "...are in the power of the tongue." When we *speak* the word, it is brought to pass by the power that we *speak* into it. In my mouth lies the power to *speak* positive things into and over my life, and what I *speak* will eventually begin to manifest!

Our words are powerful, and we must ALWAYS monitor what comes out of our mouth. If you *speak* negative things out of your mouth, then NOW is the time for you to shift what you've been *speaking* in order to make your life better! Once you tap into just how much authority has been given to you, you tap into a better future for you and those connected to you. It's a shame that many of us and people around us have suffered simply because of what we have spoken out of our mouths! When I was growing up, I used to hear people say all the time that "When you know better, you do better!" Now that you know just how much power is in your mouth, my question to you is simple: What are *you* going to do from this point forward?

I want you to do an evaluation of your life right now. What have you negatively created with words from your own mouth? The same power that you used to create your negative circumstances is the same power that you can tap into to create a positive circumstance for you and those connected to you.

I'm convinced that everything in my life is now turning for the better. Yes, I've made my mistakes by speaking the wrong things, but I PROMISE you things have ALREADY begun to shift. All it took was for me to attend Convocation in Memphis, TN hosted by Chief Apostle D. DeWayne Rudd and the Deeper Revelation International Ministries. The teachings on creative powers inspired, challenged, and encouraged me! They literally gave me a deeper revelation and activated a level which has now shifted my entire life! It was as if God spoke directly to me.

I realized the creative powers that God gave to me. I've always had this power, but I was not tapping into it! It's kind of funny because, even as I write this, I'm reminded of a conversation I had with a Pastor friend of mine. He told me the doctor gave him a negative report about the future of his eyesight and vision. The doctor told him that he could and would eventually go blind because of his condition.

So, he began to prepare and learn all that he could about the bible in case he could not read anymore! I'm so glad he shared that information with me. I stopped him and said,

"No sir. You are NOT about to receive that diagnosis and speak to me about it. You are going to use your creative powers to shift this very situation for the better!" I told him that **HE WILL HAVE WHAT HE SPEAKS**. If he continues to speak that, then that's going to be the condition he creates for himself. He burst out laughing and said, "You know what, bro? You're right." I reminded him of how much power and authority we have.

I am now determined to not let ANYBODY come into my presence and speak negative words over their situation or even over my own. I'm making it my business to let them know just how powerful they are if they don't know it! Why suffer with some things when we don't really have to?

I often think of people who receive life threatening diagnoses from the doctor. Many of them have died or will die prematurely because they simply leave that doctor's office or hospital stating the negative report given to them. In turn, most of them continue speaking the negative report until they lose all hope of ever being healed again. Chief Apostle D. DeWayne Rudd said it best: "What you continually think about and speak about you will eventually bring about!" So regardless of what negative report you receive from the doctor or anyone else, my question to you would be "Whose report will you believe?" Hmmm...

Why continue hearing messages on faith and healing if you don't really believe that it can happen for you? We must learn to speak those things that are in alignment with God's word only. We face enough trials, tests, and troubles. Why would we want to add more to it by speaking other negative things upon ourselves?! Whatever you want to see changed, try speaking it every day and watch what happens! Even as I type this now, I'm excited for you! If you begin to speak those things into existence, life will get better for you! Just speak and watch God manifest THROUGH YOU!

In hopes of hearing from different people on this subject, I posted a question on Facebook: Why do you need the Lord to Work on your mouth? Here is some of the feedback that I received:

- "Curses and blessings cannot come out the same mouth."

- "Because it's unruly and full of deadly poison"

- "I would say because I often speak negatively about my situations and about myself."

- "Because what sometimes comes out the mouth devours people...mostly when they are angry."

- "Negativity!"

- "Lord, work on my mouth so that what comes out is not predicated on how I feel but it is manifested from God's will. So, I don't orally abort my assignment, purpose, and destiny, or cause question how competent my character is or commit spiritual suicide on either end due to immature linguistics. Lord work on my mouth!"

- Because Life and death is in the power of the tongue. I try to speak life every day and not try to hurt anyone with this mouth of mine. Even when trials come and when someone says hurtful things about me but instead of cursing them out, I try to say positive things and let God do what I can't do...Don't let No words come from my mouth that is not God's word! Amen."

The scripture says that *From the abundance of the heart, the mouth speaketh* (Luke 6:45b KJV) If you want to get to the root of the mouth and what comes out of it, the heart is really what needs the work. "The mouth is only a branch of what is in the heart!" (Just a thought...)

My Prayer:

God, in the name of Jesus,

I thank You for the person that is reading this book right now. I pray now that You would touch them mightily in the name of Jesus. I pray that You would touch their heart, mind, and spirit so that they may align with Your word and Your will for their life. Father God, I pray that You would lead them in all truth as they open their mouths to speak. I pray that as they speak it would be a representation of who You are and what You mean to them.

God, I bind the enemy now that would prompt them to speak any ill word or negativity over their life or the life of another. Let every negative spoken word and work be eradicated and cast back to the pits of hell from whence it came. I thank You now that you have replaced negative speaking with positive words and words of truth.

I thank You now that great results shall

manifest now because of their awareness to only speak those things that are in alignment with Your word and Your will. As they embark upon this new season and lifestyle of only speaking life, allow your blessings to overtake them abundantly in Jesus' name I pray!

Amen

Chapter 4

Lord, Work on My Middle

What? Know ye not that your body is the temple of the Holy Ghost, which is in you, which ye have of God, and ye are not your own? For ye are bought with a price: therefore, glorify God in your body, and in your spirit, which are God's.

~ I Corinthians 6:19-20 (KJV)

OK. Here we go!!! I don't even know where to begin as it relates to this topic! This is one of the least talked about subjects in the church. Although many people are struggling in their flesh, (the "flesh struggle" as I call it), it is not getting the proper attention in the church as it should. The topic of sex and sexual struggles is taboo in the church. Many people just don't want to take the time and/or energy to address it because of the embarrassment that sometimes comes from the discussion.

Others don't want to address these issues because they are still struggling in these areas themselves.

One thing that I've found out is that although sex is hardly talked about in the church, it is EVER MORE expressed through folk in the church through deeds and actions. Growing up in the church, I never heard messages preached about sex or sexual struggles. I also never heard bible studies taught on such things, but I knew that there were a lot of "suspicious" things happening! Young girls were popping up pregnant everywhere, and young boys were becoming teenage fathers. These teenagers hardly knew how to drive a car. Plus, many baby daddies were nowhere to be found. With so many pregnancies, diseases, and death that have invaded our land, this is a subject that must be discussed even if it makes us cringe! If preachers would be transparent, then the people will stop hiding and start healing! It's time for the healing to begin!

Everything begins with a seed. I say that all the time. When I see people who are promiscuous and involved in many different lifestyles, I understand that this "thing" started somewhere. With the population on the rise of those struggling sexually and with their orientation, we can't be naïve enough to believe that these numbers are just rising because it's "the time that we're living in!" NO! NO! NO! NO! NO! Most times it's because somewhere a seed was planted and never addressed or uprooted. The curiosity about sex and what sex feels like has taken many children, who are now adults, on the rollercoaster of a lifetime. Many think that they can play around, experience, or experiment different things sexually once or twice and be done. On the contrary, let me just tell you now: RUN, RUN, RUN, RUN, and RUN! It's a TRICK!

"The Seed"

The struggle of lust and perversion comes from a seed that has been planted and never uprooted. This is a REAL struggle. This spirit can be a direct result from childhood masturbation and exploration. Many children, teenagers, and adults have experienced or will experience masturbation. Some say that it is a sin while others say that it is natural. Whatever your thoughts on this, it can open your mind and your thoughts and lead to other sexual experiences that can take you on a rollercoaster path.

Another way the enemy gets in is through planting seeds of lust and perversion through pornographic materials such as videos, magazines and even now through comics. IT'S A SET UP! This is a set-up because pornography stimulates your mind and your body which causes many to want the gratification of what they are beholding. As a result, this spirit becomes hungry and NEVER satisfied. You seek more gratification as this spirit is fed which eventually leads to actions. I was always told that if you play around with fire, eventually you'll get burned.

Satan has so many devices that he is using to destroy individuals! It's a sad thing for those of us in the church because there's not enough teaching and preaching in the church on this subject to continually keep us aware of these devices.

What do you do when you know church and church lingo but don't know how to confront this secret demon of lust and perversion? What do you do when you know what the Word says about certain actions but cannot control the sexual impulses when they happen? What do you do when you know the right thing to do, but the wrong thing keeps happening uncontrollably?

When I'm struggling with my flesh along with the spirit of lust and perversion, I don't need another preacher to tell me that God's about to bless me. I don't need another promotion or title in the church. I don't need another high service where everybody is bucking, running, dancing, shouting, and transferring spirits. HELL...I NEED TO BE DELIVERED! Now I know I just lost ALL of the deep folks when I said "hell," but if deliverance doesn't take place, then you will be delivered to hell!

I've had deep conversations with others about the struggle of sex, sexuality, lust, and perversion. You would be amazed that most of the people who are struggling want to be delivered. Many have prayed and asked God to take it away, and it yet remains a part of their life. Many have fasted for twenty-one, forty-one, or however many days that they felt the need to but still have not been delivered. Let me suggest to you that you are not alone and that there is still hope for you.

Romans 7:14-21 (KJV) speaks about this constant struggle between spirit and flesh:

For we know that the law is spiritual: but I am carnal, sold under sin. For that which I do I allow not: for what I would, that do I not; but what I hate, that do I. If then I do that which I would not, I consent unto the law that it is good. Now then it is no more I that do it, but sin that dwelleth in me. For I know that in me (that is, in my flesh,) dwelleth no good thing: for to will is present with me; but how to perform that which is good I find not. For the good that I would I do not; but the evil which I would not, that I do. Now if I do that I would not, it is no more I that do it, but sin that dwelleth in me. I find then a law, that, when I would do good, evil is present with me.

It amazes me how the church runs from this topic. We will mention fornication (sex before marriage) and adultery (sex outside of marriage), but it ends there. There are no in depth talks or teachings about the 'nitty gritty' of it all. Many of you are reading this book and are struggling right now because of a generational curse. Although some of you feel like you are the only one in your family struggling sexually, nine times out

John Jackson

of ten, you're not. I've been able to trace back certain spirits of my family, and I even recognized certain spirits dominating other families that ignited the generational curses. These curses and spirits must be called out by name and broken over our lives and the lives of our children. I never want my children to struggle with the spirit of lust and perversion as I did. Therefore, I'm constantly in prayer that God would cover and keep them away from what I had to go through and endure.

If the seeds of lust and perversion are not uprooted, each will spill over into your life and begin to affect the foundations you have built. You have to make up your mind to let it go and fight for your deliverance. I never said that it would be easy, but I can guarantee you it's worth the fight. Friendships, relationships, families, governments, nations, marriages, and even churches have been destroyed because of the lack of control to allow God to work on "the middle." When seeking deliverance, the seed of lust and perversion must be called out in prayer. Call it what it is, bind them up, and loose the spirit of holiness and righteousness. Regardless of what the enemy has told you about yourself, please know that God has a plan

63

for your life.

"It All Started Way Back When..."

I have grown up in church ALL my life, but I experienced things that no child should ever have to face. At the tender age of five, my experience with sexual molestation started. Once I turned fourteen, I continued and even consented to sexual acts with adults. This didn't make my situation any better, but I did what I thought at the time was the right thing to do. I kept the molestation to myself because I didn't want to upset my mom and other family members. After all, I was in church and on the outside, it appeared that everything was going great. I joked and hid my pain even though I was screaming for help on the inside.

I never said a mumbling word to any adult or school counselors except for once. I went and told the mother and sister of my abuser. I was told that I was a liar and that I better not ever tell anybody else. This was the beginning of a long life of internalization. Since everyone thought I was vying for attention, I just shut down and dealt with the rejection quietly. Although I kept this a secret for many years, there were times when I did open up to a few of my friends about it only to find that some of them had experienced the same thing.

This was not a one-person thing. It was family, family friends, school officials, church folk and strangers. Now as I write this section of the book, many of you may be waiting for me to call out names of my abusers, but that is not necessary. I have forgiven them and so has God. That's all that matters at this point of my life. I believe that what was done to me for many years can now be a blessing and help to someone else if I would just do what I'm doing now and that's to write about it!

My sexual abuse started me on a road that would cause me so much pain. I felt violated and worthless, but I really didn't know who to talk to about it because it seemed as if everybody wanted to abuse me! This was a trick of the enemy. I began to struggle sexually and began a life of exploration. I began to act out silently and sleep around with MANY different people which resulted in me getting a 14 - year - old white girl pregnant. She miscarried on December 24, 1994. God knew that I was definitely not ready to become a father at that time.

I would often sit, cry, and pray that God would send my dad to me to protect me from all the sick people out there who were taking advantage of me at such a young age. It never happened. As a result, I continued to cover up my abuse and struggle privately with no help from the church or anyone else. I wanted my life to appear perfect to everyone and my family, but honestly, I was hurting badly. I was seeking someone who could look into my young eyes and just ask me a question: **"John, is anybody messing with you?"**

I went to church Sunday after Sunday, revival after revival, musical after musical, but I never heard anybody talk about sex. I was a young boy who was caught up in a struggle that I shouldn't have been in, but no one took the time to care. To me, it was as if I had become a target. I started questioning myself. Was I drawing this attention to myself? Was I initiating my perpetrators? Was I throwing off a sign that said I wanted it? Was I being punished? Was this right? Was this wrong? I had a million questions going through my head. The place I was seeking help from was the same place where I kept falling deeper and deeper into pain: the church! Smh...

I prayed to God sometimes to not wake up the next day. I didn't want to face or deal with my struggles any longer.

I began to use sex as the answer to all of my problems. The more I got it, the more I wanted it! Having sex with different people made me feel loved, wanted, and accepted. Many of you reading this book right now know exactly what I'm talking about. You are either experiencing this right now, or you have experienced it in the past! No one else may be talking to you about it but let me be the first to tell you that PROMISCUITY is NOT the answer! It's a trap that is set up by Satan to destroy you and bring destruction to everything connected to you: *The thief cometh not, but for to steal, and to kill, and to destroy; I have come that they might have life, and that they might have it more abundantly.* (John 10:10 KJV)

Spirits can connect without even speaking a word! It's amazing now to think back that many of my hookups were made without even opening my mouth. It was because of connected spirits! Trust me when I say that a "ho" knows another "ho" whenever they are in each other's presence. I'm not amazed by all these super-spiritual people who consistently attempt to belittle the unsaved. Many times, I can look at them and already know that they're doing more than a "He-ka-ma-shama" (No pun intended).

Many of us can testify that we have looked for love in all the wrong places. We thought that we could find love through greets, meets, and sheets. That is so far from the truth. Most girls/women think that if they give themselves to a boy/man sexually then it will keep him and make him love her. That is so not the case! The spirit of lust cares nothing about "love." Its only desire is to fulfill its sexual gratification and then move on to the next victim. If he/she really loves you, then keep your legs closed and your zipper zipped. Trust me: time will tell. Don't get me wrong, sex is good. However, it's great when it's done in the covenant of marriage.

Many people never truly open up because of the fear of rejection from those they talk to about their struggle. If people cannot come to the church for help, then where else can they turn to? We have got to be a people that learn to embrace people wherever they are and love them as Christ loves them! Oh my, where would I be if Apostle Shawn L. Stephens would have turned me away and never embraced me and loved me beyond it all? Thanks Sir!

I wish I could go back in my past and erase all of the mess and people that I willingly and unwillingly gave myself to sexually. I can't change my past, but I'm assured through God that I could reach someone else if I opened up about my own failures, shortcomings, and struggles even in my past. To God be the Glory! If I had only known then what I know now, I wouldn't have endured the many setbacks and trials in my life. Honestly, someone is reading this book now, and you are reflecting on what you did, who you did, and when you did it. Therefore, if no one has ever told you this before let me be the first to tell you: God still loves you. Yes, He will forgive you. Yes, He will cleanse you from all unrighteousness! He also can still use you. All you have to do is ask for the Lord to work on your middle!

Many people are struggling sexually because this is a spirit that has no barrier. Lust does not care if you are black or white, rich or poor, educated or uneducated, young or old. If delivery does not happen from this spirit of perversion, it can and will eventually destroy you.

"Restoration Is Still Possible"

I don't care if you've slept with only one person, 100 people, or 1,000 people. Our God is a forgiving God. He will heal and restore you from all your hurt and pain.

Many of you need to honestly plead to God to work on your middle. There's no need to be ashamed if you are struggling. I believe our biggest problem in the church is we feel like we have to appear before the people as if we have no issues and/or struggles. As a result, we privately try to deal with these things alone and they eventually destroy us because we never open up about them. So, what happens when our private struggle becomes public shame? Hmmmm...Now that will preach right there all by itself!

Ask God to help you with your struggle

and constantly depend on him to do just that. As you are fleeing and exiting out of this life of lust and perversion, you will see all kinds of signs that will be begging you to stay. People from your past, thoughts from your experiences, and all of the above will try to resurface. However, you must RUN, RUN, and continue to RUN! Your very life and your soul are depending on you. Others are depending on you too, but most of all GOD IS depending on you. And yes, I'M DEPENDING ON YOU AS WELL!

As you begin your new journey from the bondage of lust and inappropriate desires, you must make sure to refrain from everything and everyone that will lure you back into that sinful place you are exiting from. This means that you must refrain from masturbation, self-gratification, pornographic materials (books, pictures, videos, and websites), and any conversation that will lead to you going back and committing the acts.

The spirit of lust is very greedy. The more you feed it, the more it will eat. This is the reason that you've got to starve that spirit. Remember that what you feed will continue to live but what you starve will die!

I am not telling you that the thoughts of lustful desires will not enter your mind. I am telling you that the sooner you cast them down, the sooner you can walk in victory.

I'm not here to beat and bash you because I know firsthand how strong the struggle is. So, if at first you don't succeed, try, try, and try again!

The enemy is going to try to make you feel that you will never be able to escape from those sinful desires, but that devil is a liar! Take one day at a time and keep progressing. There's a famous quote that says, "The only way to eat an elephant is by eating it one bite at a time." As you begin your journey to sexual freedom from sinful desires, you will begin to see that the things you once desired are no longer appealing and desiring to you. Even if you happen to fall and commit those acts again, you will quickly discover that it just doesn't feel the same!

Even as a Man of God, an Apostle, a preacher, a husband, a father, a son, a brother, or whatever title I've walked under, I've had to struggle with my flesh! I'm no

different from the brother sitting in the pew.
I wake up in the morning just like the next
brother! When the midnight hours come, I
have to cast the devil out of my mind just
like the next saint! I'm no different, and
that's what I want you to understand. I don't
want people to look at me and think that I
wake up speaking in tongues and go to bed
speaking in tongues. No ma'am and no sir!
It's a battle for me as well, but I'm now
learning to get the victory over this devil.
He's used me enough. If walls could talk, I
would truly be scared of what they would
say. This may seem a little comical, but it's
REAL TALK!

I love to sing and write music. Much of
the music that I write is inspirational and
encouraging, but there is one song that I
wrote in particular that was very personal to
me because it was my prayer to God. This
song was a song about my flesh. I was
struggling and needed help and so I
resorted to what gave me therapy: my
music. I am praying that this song blesses
nations and you:

Lord work on me for
my desire is to be free.
Lord free me totally

I want to be used by you.
Lord work on me,
I wanna be the vessel
that you've called me to be,
But sometimes my flesh
tries to get the best of me.
But yet I claim, yes, I claim victory!

I pray that the words of this song bless you as much as it has already been a blessing to me.

In the midst of your struggle, pray to God and ask him to work on you. Don't be afraid to reach out to someone for help if you are being abused and/or struggling sexually or with your sexuality. Matter of fact, I encourage you to do so and do it as soon as possible (ASAP). Don't wait and let the spirit of lust overtake you. Instead, deal with it from the root. The sooner you confront it, the sooner you will conquer it! There are some people out there who will instruct you and pray you through until you walk in total freedom.

Many of the people who were talking about me and trying to embarrass me in public were the ones trying to sleep with me in private! Where do they do that at?

Everywhere! I think one of the worst things for a person to do is to get with "the crowd" and belittle another person. However, they privately try to sleep with them because they think they know what their weakness is. Lord, help the Church!

I'm so happy today because I learned how to open up after all of those years. Now I can talk about my sexual struggles and sexual abuse. It was only when I began to talk about them that I got to the root of my pain and realized that it was never my fault!

Don't allow the enemy to make you suffer and/or struggle any longer. Make a commitment today that from this day on you will move forward to your freedom. The road to recovery can be a lonesome road but be assured that YOU ARE NOT ALONE! There is a God walking you through the entire process. He sees you in your valley and comforts you in your weariness. So keep walking until you walk out of it.

Find you a place of worship as often as possible. Get into His word daily. Continue to maintain a prayer life. Ask God for His delivering power. Find a good bible teaching ministry and settle yourself there. Your recovery process will be easier. God wants to make us HOLY and WHOLE, and it does not matter how long you've been in it. He can and will still set you free!

Many will try to destroy your today and your tomorrow with your past, but God is still faithful. He will cover and strengthen you through it all. Many people will never forget what they heard or knew about you, but God will see you through to your victory! Many people will talk but let them keep talking. It will only make you stronger in the process. Allow the Lord to work on you so you can help someone else in the future.

If I only reach one person with my life story or this book, I've done my duty. I'm not crazy enough to believe that this type of stuff no longer occurs. While you are reading this book right now, somebody is being fondled, molested, abused, struggling with their sexuality, and caught up in sexual sin right now.

To the man, woman, boy, or girl reading this book, please know that God knows your issue. He is only waiting on you to call it out and give it to Him. Tell the devil that he is a liar and that he will no longer have dominion over you. The devil is not on the mortgage papers of your life so KICK HIM OUT!

Prayer:

God in the name of Jesus,

I pray now for the person reading this book that's struggling in the area of lust, perversion, and sexual sin. Forgive them for their sins. Deliver and set them free now by the power of the Holy Ghost!

I come now against the spirit of lesbianism, homosexuality, perversion, and lust. I call you out now in the name of Jesus and speak deliverance over the life of this reader. Satan you have no power, no authority, and no victory over this reader and the blood of Jesus is against you now. I bind every spirit that's not like God and uproot it now from the spirit of this reader. I loose the spirit of liberty, freedom, and deliverance now.

They shall no longer struggle. They shall walk in total victory. They shall be just whom the Father has created them to be. I thank You, God, now that this reader is a testimony of one who has escaped the destructive end of the enemy and will tell forth Your glory of how You brought deliverance into their life. Thank You for looking beyond their faults and seeing their every need. We declare and decree now that this reader will never be the same in Jesus' name.

Amen

If you have received this prayer, you are on your way to recuperation and recovery. God is well pleased. Don't look back! Instead, move forward! Run from everything that seeks to pull you backwards into your old self! This is the season that you move forward in Jesus' name!

I pray that you have been blessed, convicted, inspired, and encouraged to live for God. I pray you be who He has created you to be before the foundations of the world. I have gone through many transitions in my life, and God has still been good to me. He continues to manifest himself in my life. You may not always dot every "I" and cross every "T" but strive daily to live Holy and upright before God. This is not the time to be self-righteous! People are hurting and seeking a true, genuine, and authentic relationship with God. You can be the help that they need in order to be drawn to Christ.

Always remember that we can never be too good, but we also can never be too bad that God cannot use us for his glory. Look at me.

As you end this book, just simply say,

LORD WORK ON ME!

LORD WORK ON MY MIND!

LORD WORK ON MY MIDDLE!

Although I'm not perfect and don't even pretend to be, please know APOSTLE JOHN "JJ" JACKSON is just a man trying to live holy. BE BLESSED, AND I LOVE YOU ALL!!!

About the Author

John "JJ" Jackson is a man after God's own heart! Born in Louisiana but raised in Arkansas, his heart for God was discovered at an early age. As his gifts were discovered, he embraced and nurtured them. Many people all across the world have been blessed to hear of this powerful, influential, and inspirational voice. What started off as just a gospel music interest quickly shifted into a passion for God's word and the people.

John uses his voice musically as well as speaking all across the world. He has appeared on popular television shows and was a finalist on season 6 of BET's Sunday Best singing competition.

His love for music can be heard in his debut single entitled, "My Future" which can be found on all digital musical outlets. His love for the God's people can be heard when he mounts a pulpit to preach and/or speak but also can be heard on the *RecoveryMode Daily Morning Inspirations* every morning at 10am CST on his social media pages Facebook @apostlejohn.jackson or on Instagram @johnjackson_sb6.

John received his high school diploma from El Dorado High School in El Dorado, AR and went on to the University of Arkansas at Pine Bluff in Pine Bluff, AR where he received a BS degree in Criminal Justice. He is the Founder/Visionary of RecoveryMode Fellowship which is rapidly impacting lives all over the United States as he deems his objective/assignment is to "SHIFT MINDS FROM CHURCH TO KINGDOM!"

Be BLESSED, Be ENCOURAGED and Be

INSPIRED by the words of John JJ Jackson.

Get Connected with Author John Jackson on Social Media

 Facebook.com/apostlejohn.jackson

 Instagram.com/johnjackson_sb6

From Breakdown to Breakthrough

Made in the USA
Columbia, SC
26 January 2022

54725620R00052